Creative Keyboard Presents

Great Literature for Piano

BAROQUE – CLASSICAL – ROMANTIC

BOOK III
INTERMEDIATE

Researched and Compiled by
GAIL SMITH

© 1993 by Mel Bay Publications, Inc., Pacific, MO. 63069.
All Rights Reserved. International Copyright Secured. B.M.I. Made and Printed in the U.S.A.

Foreword

In early 19th-century Germany, the purchase of a piano commanded the interest of the new owner's entire community. The German family that ordered the piano first made a down-payment in cash. Upon completion of the piano, they paid for the balance in corn, wheat, potatoes, poultry, and firewood.

On the day that the piano was to be delivered to the new owner, the town held a festival. A band of musicians headed the procession, followed by the proud piano maker, who was borne on the shoulders of his assistants. Flowers and wreaths decorated the horse-drawn wagon which held the precious piano. Musicians, schoolmasters, and dignitaries marched in the rear.

At last the piano arrived at its destination. The delighted new owners greeted the procession warmly. The local clergyman said a prayer, blessing the new instrument as well as its craftsmen. The mayor delivered an address; the schoolmaster, doctor, and other dignitaries gave speeches. Finally, the men's chorus sang. When the piano was properly installed in its new home, everyone enjoyed a banquet and danced in celebration of this happy occasion.

In contrast, today the purchase of a piano seems no longer to be a cause for festivity and joy. Unfortunately, our generation takes such purchases for granted. We have forgotten what a treasure and gift a piano can be. We have also forgotten what a treasure and gift the great composers have given us through their beautiful musical compositions for the piano.

This new piano literature series rediscovers the "rare jewels" of piano literature. After years of research and meticulous assessment of the composers of Baroque, Classical, and Romantic music, this exciting "quest for the best" has led to a new series of eight graded books . . . all containing original compositions by the masters.

The series begins with the most easily mastered compositions, progressing to the more advanced and musically difficult selections. Pianists on all levels will enjoy this challenging, thorough, and diversified collection of piano music. In addition, an interesting biographical sketch of each composer will make these selections more meaningful to the student.

Just as flowers and wreaths decorated the horse-drawn wagon that delivered the new piano to the fortunate German villager, likewise flowers and wreaths decorate each book in this series. They serve as a reminder for us all to treasure each selection we learn and to be thankful for our magnificent musical heritage.

Gail Smith

Note to Teachers

The pieces selected in each book are in approximate order of difficulty. They are not necessarily in chronological order. Before the selections of each new composer, there is a short biographical sketch of that composer. In addition, many include a pictorial representation, as well.

Book One . . . . late primary-level and early elementary-level pieces

Book Two . . . . harder elementary pieces

Book Three . . . . medium-level or intermediate pieces

Book Four . . . . moderately difficult pieces

Book Five . . . . difficult pieces

Book Six . . . . very difficult pieces

Book Seven . . . . musically advanced sonatas

Book Eight . . . . musically advanced longer pieces

Contents
Book Three

Jeremiah Clarke

(c. 1659 – December 1, 1707)

Clarke was an English organist and composer at the Chapel Royal. In 1704, he was made joint organist with William Croft. He is remembered most for his "Trumpet Voluntary," but composed many orchestral, chamber, vocal, and keyboard works.

Jigg

Jeremiah Clarke

Georg Philipp Telemann
(March 14, 1681 – June 25, 1767)

This German composer was most popular in his day, and in recent years he has been "rediscovered." In 1708 he was appointed Kapellmeister at Eisenach, where he became a friend of Johann Sebastian Bach. He was godfather to Bach's third son, Carl Philipp Emanuel Bach.

Fantasia

Georg Philipp Telemann

Adagio

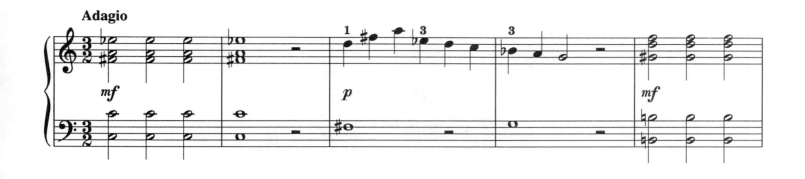

D.C. al Fine

Johann Pachelbel
(September 1, 1653 – March 3, 1706)

This magnificent German organist and composer held many important positions during his lifetime. Pachelbel was one of Bach's early models in composition. He taught Bach's older brother. His *Hexachordun Apollinis (1699)* (six sets of variations) is considered his best work. Everyone is playing the "Pachelbel Canon in D."

Gavotte and Variations

Johann Pachelbel

Var. II. (Sarabande)
Andante

Johann Sebastian Bach
(March 21, 1685 – July 28, 1750)

The great Johann Sebastian Bach was born in German Eisenach. His brother became his teacher when his parents died when he was 10. Though so young, he longed each day for songs more difficult to play. These songs his brother did forbid and from Johann his music hid! But through the cupboard's latticed door Bach reached the tempting music score. And every moonlit night he wrote the precious copy note by note. Very secretly he learned and played, and then his brother was quite dismayed! But master of the fugue became, which won for him immortal fame. And though at last he lost his sight, his faith in God made darkness light.

Allegro

Johann Sebastian Bach

Gigue in A Major
Friedemann Bach Book

J.S. Bach

21

Henry Purcell
(c. 1659 – November 21, 1695)

Purcell was adopted by his uncle after his father died. He spent his childhood as a choir-boy of the Chapel Royal. When his voice changed, Purcell worked in Westminster Abbey as a music copyist and studied composition with John Blow. At the age of 20, Purcell succeeded Blow as organist of Westminster Abbey. Purcell married and had six children. He composed church anthems for cathedral services, numerous plays, and secular keyboard music. The Purcell Society was formed in 1876 to study, publish, and perform his works.

Prelude
from Suite V

Purcell

Domenico Scarlatti
(October 26, 1685 – July 23, 1757)

Scarlatti was a great harpsichord virtuoso and composer who is the "Father of Modern Piano Playing." He introduced crossing of hands, the rapid repetition of a note, and far-flung arpeggio passages in his more than 600 harpsichord pieces. He played in a contest with Handel at the palace in Rome. It was a tie in harpsichord playing, while Handel proved to be the better organist! Scarlatti and Handel remained friends throughout their lifetime.

Sonata
L. 90

Domenico Scarlatti

30

Francois Couperin
(November 10, 1668 – September 12, 1733)

Couperin was a skillful harpsichord player and published a method of touch and ornamentation execution in the performance of his pieces for harpsichord. It is known that Bach studied this method and even copied some of it in his courantes. Around 1689 Couperin married Marie Anne Ansault, and they had two daughters.

The Startled Bird

Francois Couperin

George Frederic Handel
(February 23, 1685 – April 14, 1759)

Handel's father, a barber–surgeon, was 63 years old when his son George Frederic was born. Because his father wanted him to have a good education and not become a musician, young Handel would have to practice secretly in the attic.

Gigue
from Suite No. 4

George Frederic Handel

Aria
from Suite No. 14

George Frederic Handel

Courante

George Frederic Handel

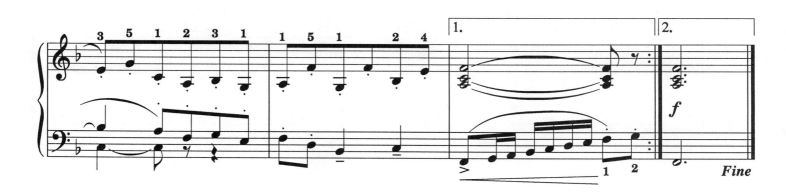

41

Allegro
from Suite No. 7

George Frederic Handel

Stephen Heller
(May 15, 1813 – January 14, 1888)

Heller was a popular pianist and composer who played in public when he was 9 years old. He became a friend of Liszt, Chopin, and Berlioz and was held in high esteem as a teacher and performer. He published a large number of piano works.

Etude

Allegretto
sempre legato ed egualmente

Stephen Heller

Etude

Allegro assai (♩ = 126)

Stephen Heller

Waltz
Op. 39, No. 16

Johann Brahms

Ludwig van Beethoven
(December 1770 – 1827)

Beethoven deserves to be called the Shakespeare of music. He reached the heights and depths of human emotion as no other composer has done. Beethoven's ability to imagine melodies and harmonies, composing even when he became deaf, underscores his genius.

Für Elise

Ludwig Van Beethoven

53

Peter Ilich Tchaikovsky
(May 7, 1840 – November 6, 1893)

Tchaikovsky studied composition with Anton Rubinstein at the St. Petersburg Conservatory. Tchaikovsky was a hard worker. Once when his teacher assigned him to write some variations, he stayed up all night and produced 200! All his life he worked for perfection and often destroyed the scores he wrote, thinking they were not good enough. In 1891, he visited America and conducted his own works at Carnegie Hall in New York City.

Mazurka
Op. 39, No. 10

Peter Tchaikovsky

Edvard Grieg
(June 15, 1843 – September 4, 1907)

Grieg's mother gave him his first piano lessons. Much of his music is based on Norwegian folk songs. After studying at the Conservatory at Leipzig, Grieg married, then began a concert tour with his wife. Nina stood beside him singing the songs he had written for her. They also played duets on the piano. They even performed for Queen Victoria at Windsor Castle. Grieg composed numerous piano works and the famous "Piano Concerto in A Minor." He also conducted his "Peer Gynt Suite" with the London Philharmonic Society.

Dance of the Elves

Edvard Grieg, Op. 12, No. 4

Molto allegro e sempre staccato M.M. ♩ = 84

Jakob Ludwig Felix Mendelssohn
(November 3, 1809 – November 4, 1847)

Mendelssohn's father was a rich banker. All distinguished musical people who passed through Berlin visited their home. On Sunday there was always an afternoon concert by Felix and his talented sister Fanny. Mendelssohn began to compose at the age of 10. He not only composed and performed his own works, but he revived the works of Johann Sebastian Bach, which had been forgotten for a hundred years.

Venetian Boat Song
Composed in 1830

Felix Mendelssohn
Op.19, No.6

Robert Alexander Schumann
(June 8, 1810 – July 1856)

To the general public, Schumann was "the husband" of Clara Wieck, concert pianist, rather than the famous composer we think of today. He wrote abundantly for the piano. He wrote numerous easier pieces for his own five children, and very difficult compositions for his wife to perform. Johann Brahms was their friend and would often baby-sit their children.

In Memoriam
Composed in memory of Mendelssohn

Allegretto molto cantabile

Robert Schumann

Knight Rupert
From "Album for the Young"

Robert Schumann
Op. 68, No. 12

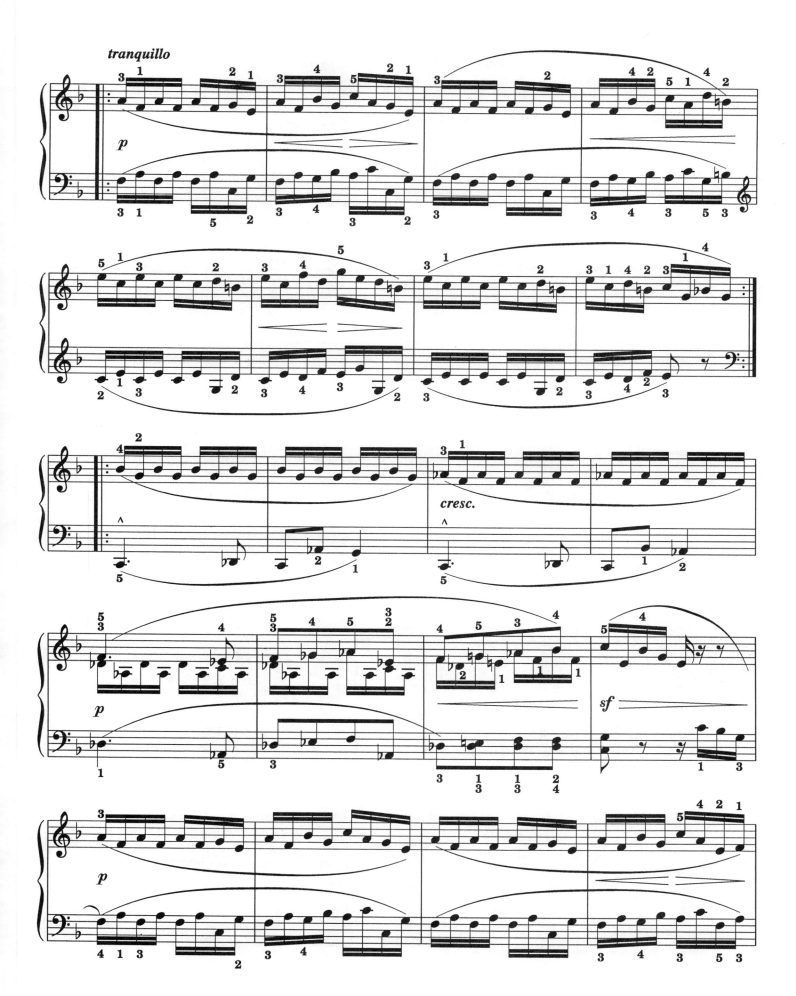

Norse Song

The Danish composer, Niels W. Gade 1817–1890

This composition uses the musical letters in Gade's name.

Robert Schumann
Op. 68, No. 41

71

Niels W. Gade
(February 22, 1817 – December 21, 1890)

This Danish composer was the son of an instrument maker. He entered the royal orchestra as a violinist, and he was a friend of Mendelssohn and Robert Schumann. His first symphony was performed in 1843 in Leipzig. He married the daughter of the composer J. P. E. Hartmann. Gade was the most famous Danish composer of the 19th century.

Ring Dance

Niels W. Gade

Jan Ladislav Dussek
(February 12, 1760 – March 12, 1812)

Dussek was a Bohemian pianist and composer who began his piano lessons at the age of 5. He became a choir-boy at Iglau and received some lessons from C. P. E. Bach, who was the second son of the great J. S. Bach. As an adult, Dussek gave a concert tour of Germany and played for Marie Antoinette. He was a remarkable piano virtuosi who is said to have been the first concert pianist to place his instrument sideways upon the platform.

O Dear What Can the Matter Be?

J. L. Dussek

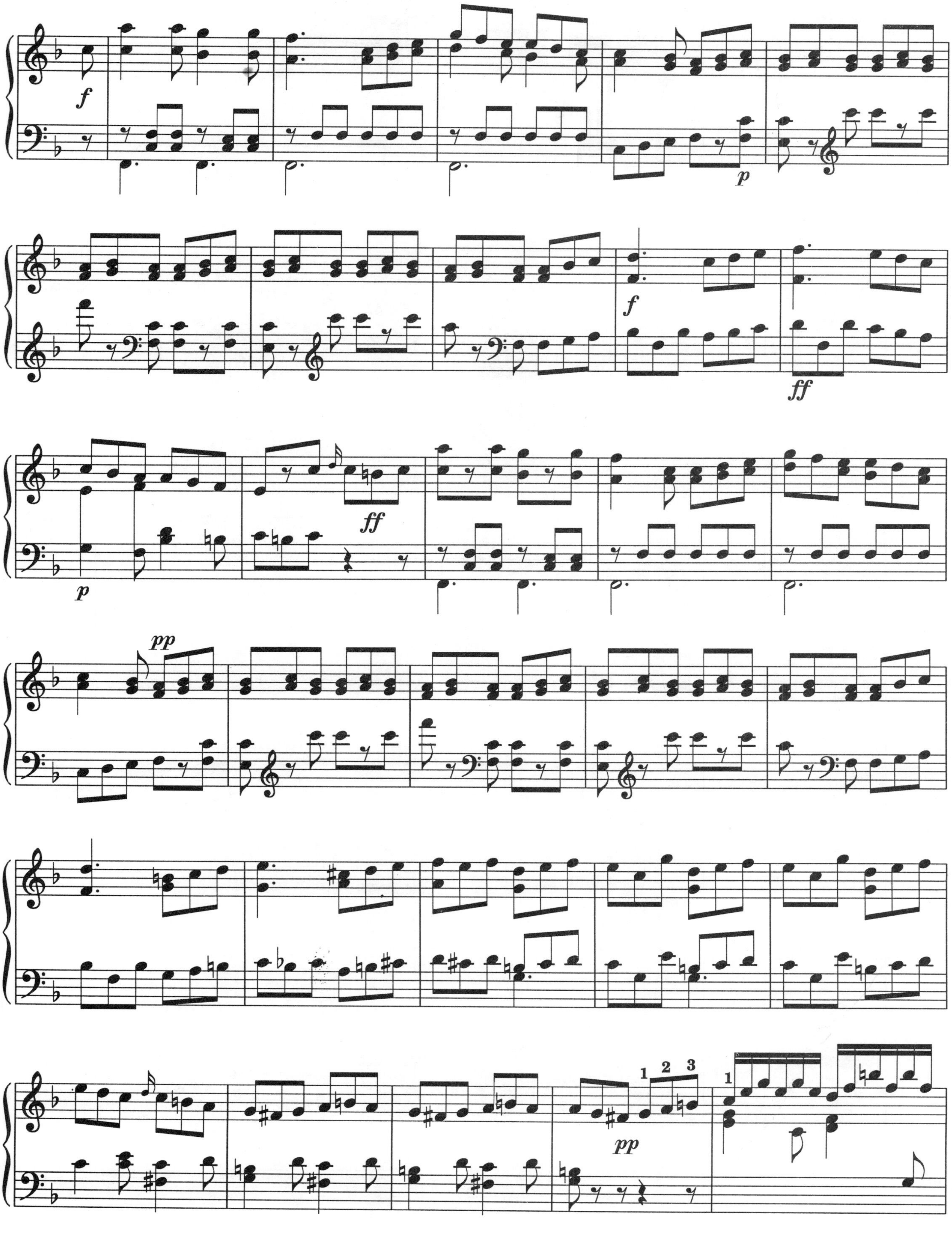
f
p
f
ff
p
ff
pp
1 2 3
1
pp

Wolfgang Amadeus Mozart
(January 27, 1756 – December 5, 1791)

Mozart and his older sister showed amazing musical talent at a very young age. Their father, Leopold, decided to commercialize their gifts and set up concert tours in many cities, including Munich, Vienna, Paris, and London. The concerts were very successful, and the children often played for royalty. Mozart began composing at age 5 and continued writing beautiful music all his life.

Theme and Variations
"Ah, vous dirai-je, Maman"

W. A. Mozart
K. 265

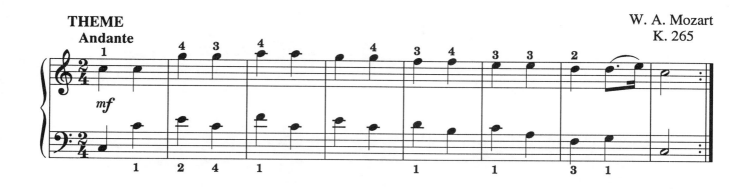

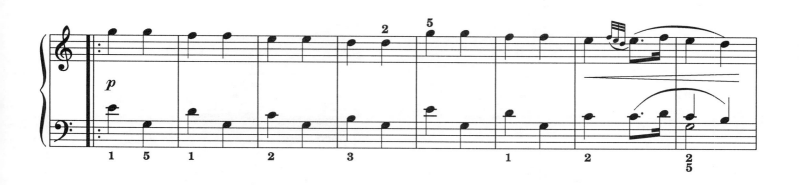

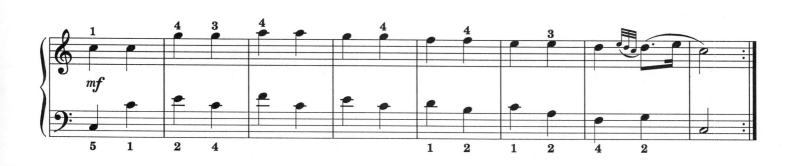

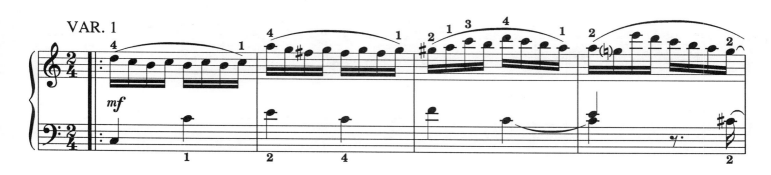

Viennese Sonatina No. 1
First Movement

Wolfgang Amadeus Mozart

Allegro brillante

Franz Joseph Haydn
(March 31, 1732 – May 31, 1809)

Haydn was the first great master of the symphony and the string quartet. He looked on his genius as a gift from above and dictated the inscription on all his scores, large and small, "In nomine Domini" at the beginning and "Laus Deo" at the end. Mozart dedicated the well-known six quartets he composed to Haydn.

Sonata
C Major

Allegro con brio

Joseph Haydn

Franz Peter Schubert
(January 31, 1797 – November 19, 1828)

Schubert was born at the house of the Red Crab near Vienna. His father was a poor schoolmaster. The family had 19 children, but only 8 lived to be adults.

When Schubert was 8 years old, his father taught him to play the violin. Next, he began singing lessons from Mr. Michael Holzer, the parish choir-master, who declared with tears in his eyes that he never before had such a pupil. Schubert's oldest brother, Ignaz, gave him piano lessons. When Schubert was 11 years old, Salieri auditioned him for the choir-boys of the Imperial Chapel. He was accepted and began his life there. In those days, a boys' school was no paradise, even when the uniform was decorated with gold lace! He endured hardships at the school; however, his music flourished. By the time he was 16 he had composed his first symphony and many other works. By the end of 1815 he had composed over 537 songs.

In the summer of 1818 Schubert became the music-teacher in the family of Count Johann Esterhazy. He was paid two gulden for each lesson that he gave the three children.

Schubert was a little man, not much over five feet tall, with fat arms and short fingers. In February 1819, a song of Schubert's was sung for the first time in public. The public loved his music and just two years later the song was published. In nine months, 800 copies were sold. His success was so great that publishers were now willing to publish others. Had Schubert been wise, his future might have become secure. However, he foolishly sold his first 12 works for 800 silver gulden ($400). One single song in Op. 4, "The Wanderer," brought its publisher upwards of $13,000 between 1822–1861. Moreover, he mortgaged his future works in the same short-sighted way.

Schubert admired the works of Beethoven very much. He composed a theme and variations and dedicated them to him. Schubert visited Beethoven twice before he died and was a torch-bearer at his funeral. A year later, on the anniversary of Beethoven's death, Schubert gave his first and only public concert.

Schubert died November 19, 1828. He had requested to be buried near Beethoven in the Great Central Cemetery of Vienna. His request was granted. The poet Grillparzer wrote the celebrated epitaph:

> Music has here buried a rich treasure
> But much fairer hopes.
> Franz Schubert lies here.
> Born January 31, 1797
> Died November 19, 1828.
> 31 years old.

Ecossaise

Franz Schubert
Op. 33

Frederic Francois Chopin
(February 22, 1809 – October 17, 1849)

Chopin's father was a French teacher. His mother was Polish. His boyhood summers were spent in the country where he heard the music of the peasants and danced the national Kujawiak. At the age of 18, his father sent him to Berlin to meet musicians and hear the music performed there. When he returned to Warsaw he composed two piano concertos, then decided to leave home for Paris. Friends went with him to a banquet in a neighboring village and there presented him with a silver cup filled to the brim with Polish soil, solemnly asking him to never forget friends and fatherland.

Prelude
Op. 28, No. 7

Frédéric Chopin

Prelude
Op. 28, No. 4

Frédéric Chopin

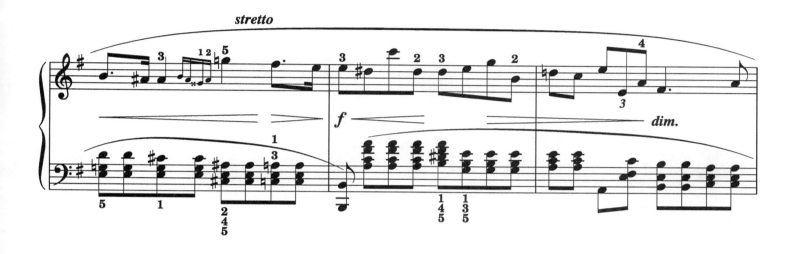

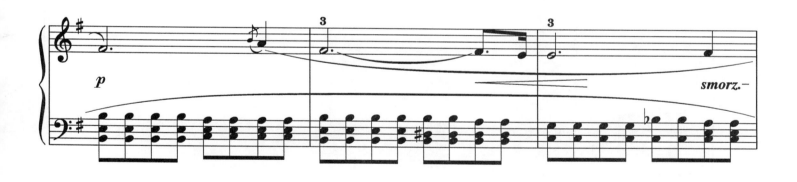

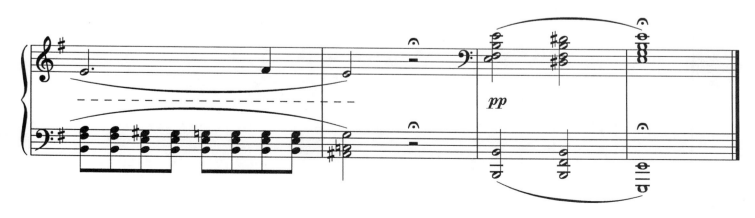